AMAZING WORD SEARCH PUZZLES for KIDS

MARK DANNA

PUZZLE
WRIGHT
PRESS

New York

For my sisters Gloria, Sally, Wendy, and Vicki,
who are amazing in their different ways

PUZZLE
WRIGHT
PRESS
New York

An Imprint of Sterling Publishing
387 Park Avenue South
New York, NY 10016

PUZZLEWRIGHT PRESS and the distinctive Puzzlewright Press logo
are registered trademarks of Sterling Publishing Co., Inc.

© 2008 by Mark Danna

This edition published in 2013.

ISBN 978-1-4549-0950-7

Distributed in Canada by Sterling Publishing
C/o Canadian Manda Group, 165 Dufferin Street
Toronto, Ontario, Canada M6K 3H6
Distributed in the United Kingdom by GMC Distribution Services
Castle Place, 166 High Street, Lewes, East Sussex, England BN7 1XU
Distributed in Australia by Capricorn Link (Australia) Pty. Ltd.
P.O. Box 704, Windsor, NSW 2756, Australia

For information about custom editions, special sales, and premium and
corporate purchases, please contact Sterling Special Sales
at 800-805-5489 or specialsales@sterlingpublishing.com.

Manufactured in the United States of America

2   4   6   8   10   9   7   5   3   1

www.puzzlewright.com

Contents

Introduction

Fun-shaped puzzles, fascinating themes, hidden messages, laugh-out-loud riddles, entertaining twists—all created by one of the top puzzlemakers in the U.S.—now that's amazing! That's what you'll find in this book: *Amazing Word Search Puzzles for Kids*.

How is this book different from other books out there? It has amazing variety, and it's well-crafted by veteran puzzlemaker Mark Danna, who cares about his work so that kids can enjoy their play. This is his thirteenth word search book for Sterling.

Tell me about the variety. First, there are the *puzzle grids*. About half are in the standard rectangular shape that kids are so familiar with. In the other half, grid letters form not a rectangle but a *picture shape* like a rocket ship, water balloon, kettledrum, tepee, or duck. Each shape is appropriate to the puzzle's theme.

There are *53 puzzles* in this book, *each with a different theme*. Themes range from movies to rhymes to MP3s to weird constellations to sneezing. And that's nothing to sneeze at!

To add spice, we've added some twists. In the two *rebus puzzles*, a little picture represents a set of letters. For example, in "Star Search" every word or phrase in the word list contains the letters S-T-A-R in consecutive order. When these letters appear in the grid (which is shaped like a big star), they appear as a little ★. So, for example, the word HEADSTART in the word list would appear in the grid as HEAD★T. In another rebus, you'll find little spinning tops inside a big top.

We're not sure we can top that, but another twist is that in two puzzles *it's up to you to come up with the word list*. You do that by using the clues given. In "All Together Now," you need to match up things that commonly come in pairs. For example, if we said CHAIR and gave you the clue T _ _ _ _, you'd say TABLE. In the puzzle titled "Word Chain," the first and last letters of the words are missing. The last letter in one word is the first letter in the next word in the chain. Additional clues come in the form of definitions.

To top it all off, *every puzzle contains a hidden message!* After you've circled all the words and phrases in the grid, read all the uncircled letters from left to right, top to bottom, to spell out a fun fact, a funny answer to a riddle, an interesting observation, or a word or phrase connected with the theme. When you try to uncover the hidden message, the letters will be in order, but you'll need to figure out how to break them into words and where to add punctuation. This puzzle-within-a-puzzle adds a level of difficulty not usually associated with word search puzzles, but it adds an extra level of fun, too. If you find it too hard, though, that's OK. You can get still get your laughs by reading the messages in the answer section.

Finding the hidden messages may be tough, but learning to solve word searches is easy. If you know how to do them, you can jump right in now. If you don't know how to do them, keep on reading and we'll tell you everything you need to know.

What's a word search puzzle? A word search is a game of hide-and-seek: we hide the words; you go seek them. Each puzzle has two main parts: a grid and a word list. The grid looks like a meaningless jumble of letters, but it actually hides all the words and phrases in the word list. As we said above, in this book about half the grids are rectangles and the other half are picture shapes.

In a word search, words and phrases always go in a straight line—horizontally, vertically, or diagonally. Horizontal words go straight across to the right or backward to the left. Vertical words go straight down or straight up. Diagonal words slant from left-to-right or right-to-left and go either upward or downward along the angle. So words can go in eight possible directions—along the lines of a plus sign (+) or a multiplication sign (×).

How do I get started? Some people look for across words first. Others begin with the long words or words with less common letters like J, Q, X, or Z. Still others start at the top of the list and work their way in order straight down to the bottom. Try a few ways and see what works best for you.

How do I mark the hidden words? Loop them, draw a straight line through them, or circle each individual letter. Whatever you choose, cross the words off the word list as you find them in the grid so as to avoid confusion. Also, be sure to be neat. Neatness will help when you're looking for all the letters that make up the hidden message.

What about punctuation? When you look for words and phrases in the grid, ignore all punctuation and spacing in the word list. For example, the phrase "EEK, A MOUSE!" in the word list would appear in the grid, in some direction, as EEKAMOUSE. Also, ignore all words in brackets like [THE] and [A]. These have been added at times to make certain word list items more understandable, but they will not appear in the grid.

Do all the circled words in the grid connect? Here and in all of Danna's books, the answer is yes. Every word in a grid crosses at least one other word, and all the words in a grid interconnect. It's much harder to make a puzzle this way, so most puzzlemakers don't do it. We think it adds elegance to the construction, so we make the extra effort.

Are some of the puzzles harder than others? For the most part, all the puzzles are about the same level of difficulty—that is, challenging but not mind-crushingly hard. Word lists generally contain 20 to 25 items—not too long but not too short. The two rebus puzzles and the two puzzles with partial word lists do require more brain power, and "Use the Paintbrush" has a full 60 hidden words to find. But feel free to jump around and do the puzzles in any order you like.

Any final words? The puzzle titles are often playful, so you may be surprised at first as to what the puzzle theme is. Be prepared to have some good, silly fun and to learn some amazing facts in the hidden messages. So enjoy it all—from the opening puzzle "In First Place" to the final one "Getting in the Last Words."

1. IN FIRST PLACE

The word FIRST can come before every item in the list below to form a common word or phrase such as FIRST-BORN or FIRST BASE. First, find and circle all these items, which are hidden in the grid. Then read the leftover letters in order to find the hidden message. It'll tell you what you just did.

BASE		LADY
BORN		MATE
CHOICE		NAME
CLASS		PAGE
COUSIN		PERSON
DAY OF SCHOOL		PLACE
DOWN		PRIZE
EDITION		QUARTER
GLANCE		STEP
HAND		THING
IMPRESSION		TIME
INNING		WORLD WAR

2. WORD SEARCH WORD SEARCH

The grid contains things that are a part of word searches in this book. The hidden message lists three of the word search shapes you'll discover as you move forward through these pages.

```
R  O  E  L  G  N  A  T  C  E  R
F  U  N  F  A  C  T  S  C  K  G
O  E  I  E  M  E  H  T  T  R  S
R  B  L  U  R  B  I  H  I  E  D
K  P  T  N  W  O  D  D  S  W  E
I  O  H  W  O  R  D  L  I  S  T
D  O  G  I  P  L  E  I  L  N  C
S  L  I  T  E  P  N  O  L  A  E
E  D  A  S  W  A  M  S  I  C  N
P  E  R  N  N  I  E  D  N  R  N
A  L  T  B  O  S  S  I  E  O  O
H  Z  S  I  A  G  S  T  S  S  C
S  Z  R  R  T  T  A  H  S  S  L
D  U  H  A  Y  L  G  I  C  A  L
K  P  H  C  R  A  E  S  D  E  A
```

ACROSS	PUZZLE
ALL CONNECTED	RECTANGLE
ANSWER	RIDDLES
BLURB	SEARCH
DIAGONAL	SHAPES
DOWN	SILLINESS
FOR KIDS	STRAIGHT LINE
FUN FACTS	THEME
GRID	TITLE
HIDDEN MESSAGE	TWISTS
LOOP	WORD LIST
PHRASES	

3. TREE-MENDOUS

Shaped like a tree, the grid contains things found in or on trees. The hidden message answers this riddle: "If you'd really like to get an oak or a maple on Halloween, what should you do?"

```
            O  W  L  S     G  O  B  K
         N  T  O  E  D  R  I  B  Y  B  A  B  C
      K  O  R  M  N  G  G  N  I  W  S  E  R  I  T
      K  C  O  M  M  A  H  A  S  G  U  B  D  K  O
         N  F  O  R  B  R  A  N  N  U  D  D  K
      S  L  E  A  F  C  U  T  T  E  R  A  N  T  S
      H  L  E  R  R  I  U  Q  S  S  O  O  N  I  U
      T  B  R     S  T  U  N  W  T  T     C  A  W
         O  T     S  U  T  O  H        T  A
               A  L  A  O  K
               L  R  L  D  N
               P  E  I  P  U
               Y  C  E  E  R
               A  A  K  C  T
               R  I  K  K  O
         R  T  T  R  B  E  R  R  Y
      E  C  H  E  S  H  I  R  E  C  A  T  E
```

ACORN	LEMON
BABY BIRD	NEST
BARK	NUTS
BEAR	OWLS
BERRY	PEAR
BUGS	SQUIRREL
CHESHIRE CAT	STRAY PLASTIC BAG
HAMMOCK	TIRE SWING
IGUANA	TREE FORT
KITE	TRUNK
KNOTHOLE	WIND
KOALA	WOODPECKER
LEAF-CUTTER ANTS	

4. LISTEN UP!

Shaped like an MP3 player, the grid contains words associated with that amazing device, which the hidden message describes in a poetic way.

```
        E   A   R   P   H   O   N   E   S
    R   A   D   N   E   L   A   C   M   Y   A
    M   C   A   S   E   E   A   D   U   R   T
    E   N   E   L   F   F   U   H   S   E   S
    O   G   I   A   R   P   I   C   I   T   A
    A   L   A   E   A   Y   T   A   C   T   C
    U   E   T   R   A   M   U   B   L   A   D
    D   N   I   S   O   R   N   L   I   B   O
    I   M   P   O   R   T   E   E   B   W   P
    O   I   O   T   T   H   S   P   R   L   E
    B   S   D   O   W   N   L   O   A   D   I
    O   E   O   H   R   T   G   Y   R   S   V
    O   A   P   P   L   E   B   A   Y   T   O
    K   R   H   A   T   A   I   S   M   P   M
    S   C   L   I   C   K   W   H   E   E   L
    O   H   R   K   T   A   S   G   N   O   S
        B   L   E   V   O   L   U   M   E
```

ALBUM ART	EARPHONES	NANO
APPLE	GAMES	PHOTOS
AUDIOBOOKS	IMPORT	PLAYBACK
BATTERY	INTERFACE	PODCAST
CABLE	IPOD	SEARCH
CALENDAR	ITUNES	SHUFFLE
CASE	MENU	SONGS
CLICK WHEEL	MOVIE	STORAGE
DOWNLOAD	MUSIC LIBRARY	VOLUME

5. OUT TO LAUNCH

Shaped like a rocket ship, the grid contains words associated with space flights. The hidden message tells what astronauts run on in the International Space Station to stay healthy and fit.

```
              N
            K W A
          T E O R E
          S N D A S
          R N T D C
        R E E N T R Y
        E T D U M U F
        V S Y O O B L
        O O S C D A I
        R O P E U M G
        S B A N L I H
        R O C K E T T
        A H E C O R H
      D M L C O L R O G
    N L T T E D H A I L I
  A S T R O N A U T T N P E
L H U L I F T O F F O A G X W
V H E R S B E N O I S S I M E
S I N T   C R E W M   A H E A
          I O R
```

ASTRONAUT	MISSION
BOOSTERS	MODULE
COUNTDOWN	MOON
CREW	NASA
DOCK	ORBIT
EXPLORE	O-RING
FLIGHT	REENTRY
KENNEDY SPACE CENTER	ROCKET
LAND	SCRUB
LAUNCH	SHUTTLE
LIFTOFF	WEIGHTLESS
MARS ROVER	

6. COLOR-FULL

The grid contains some unusual colors of minerals. The hidden message contains three more of these colors, each of them two words in length.

```
M  R  O  T  S  T  S  U  D  R  E
C  L  O  U  D  P  I  N  K  V  O
I  A  A  S  U  I  O  N  I  T  A
G  R  S  S  N  P  U  H  T  N  V
W  O  L  L  E  Y  C  E  T  Z  A
A  C  J  S  O  R  R  E  L  U  L
T  N  A  P  R  I  L  G  L  O  W
E  O  S  L  S  T  B  E  G  I  L
R  Y  U  S  I  E  H  C  M  R  A
F  N  E  O  N  C  A  R  R  O  T
A  A  K  C  Q  B  O  F  U  N  N
L  C  O  G  I  W  T  A  O  G  M
L  R  O  N  K  U  M  Q  U  A  T
K  G  R  A  P  E  M  I  S  T  M
I  N  B  E  E  S  W  A  X  E  T
```

APRIL GLOW	IRON GATE
AZTEC YELLOW	KUMQUAT
BEESWAX	LASER LEMON
BROOK	LAVA
CALICO	LOG CABIN
CANYON CORAL	NEON CARROT
CHIVE	OTTER
CLOUD PINK	POND
CORK	SEA FOAM
DUNE	SORREL
DUST STORM	TWIG
GRAPE MIST	WATERFALL

7. YIKES!

Wow! The grid contains words and phrases that commonly end with an exclamation point! The hidden message contains two more such phrases: the first one said by a parent, and the second one said in reply by a kid.

```
E  E  S  T  N  A  C  I  S  G  G
O  T  O  U  D  Y  E  O  U  U  E
H  C  U  O  E  R  L  R  R  O  T
C  O  L  H  P  M  T  T  P  H  O
O  I  E  C  P  F  T  S  R  M  U
W  H  A  T  A  N  I  D  I  O  T
A  U  V  A  R  I  L  R  S  T  O
B  R  E  W  T  H  U  N  E  H  F
U  R  M  U  E  E  O  T  E  A  H
N  Y  E  I  R  L  Y  O  O  T  E
G  U  A  H  E  P  Y  N  R  S  R
A  P  L  A  W  T  H  I  E  A  E
S  L  O  W  D  O  W  N  W  L  Y
Y  O  N  D  O  N  T  D  O  I  T
U  E  E  K  A  M  O  U  S  E  N
```

COWABUNGA!	LEAVE ME ALONE!
DON'T DO IT!	OH, NO!
EEK, A MOUSE!	OUCH!
FIRE!	SLOW DOWN!
GET OUT OF HERE!	SURPRISE!
HELP!	THAT'S A LIE!
HOORAY!	WATCH OUT!
HURRY UP!	WE'RE TRAPPED!
I CAN'T SEE!	WHAT AN IDIOT!
I WIN!	WHY YOU LITTLE... !

8. FINGER FOOD

The grid contains foods that you eat with your fingers. The hidden message is a funny word of advice about what you should never eat.

```
S  E  I  R  R  E  H  C  T  A  N
B  I  W  S  T  U  N  A  E  P  N
U  N  R  C  Y  T  C  H  I  O  H
F  W  A  O  I  O  O  Z  L  T  C
F  O  P  R  E  T  Z  E  L  A  E
A  R  N  N  D  A  M  G  R  T  L
L  B  E  O  I  R  I  B  S  O  E
O  B  G  N  E  F  I  G  H  C  R
W  G  E  T  C  R  F  T  R  H  Y
I  H  A  H  A  H  N  U  I  I  S
N  W  Y  E  O  U  F  R  M  P  T
G  P  I  C  K  L  E  R  P  S  I
S  N  R  O  C  P  O  P  I  H  C
H  A  M  B  U  R  G  E  R  E  K
E  A  D  H  C  I  W  D  N  A  S
```

BROWNIE	PICKLE
BUFFALO WINGS	PIZZA
CELERY STICKS	POPCORN
CHERRIES	POTATO CHIPS
CORN ON THE COB	PRETZEL
FRENCH FRIES	RIBS
HAMBURGER	SANDWICH
HOT DOG	SHRIMP
MUFFIN	TACO
OREO	WATERMELON
PEANUTS	WRAP

9. HEADRESTS

Shaped like a tepee, the grid contains places where you might sleep or rest. The hidden message offers one more such place, where there's plenty of fresh air and a wonderful view.

```
                I       Q       N
                  I   U   M
                    N O A
                  A N N O E
                  P S S R M
              E I L E T O H
              O O T T L H N
            N D L A H E E F I
            G E E E U L L T H
          E H S D U T N I T O D
          S K C A R R A B R S M
        C C H O U S E B O A T A K
        A M R O D       M I E W C
      B B E R L         L L G A T
      H I E S G         E T I H A
      T N E T I         R R W S S
```

BACK SEAT
BARRACKS
CABIN
CASTLE
DORM
HOSTEL
HOTEL
HOUSEBOAT
IGLOO
INN

LODGE
MANSION
MOBILE HOME
MOTEL
QUONSET HUT
SHACK
SHELTER
TENT
TRAILER
WIGWAM

10. TALKING ANIMALS

The list on this page contains 20 animal sounds as they're spoken in different languages. Find those sounds in the duck-shaped grid on the facing page. Then read the hidden message to discover how one animal sound in the U.S. means something quite different somewhere else.

Dogs
Hebrew: HAV HAV!
Japanese: WON-WON!
Swahili: HU HU HU HUUU!

Ducks
Chinese: GA-GA!
French: GUAHN GUAHN!

Frogs
Russian: KVA-KVA!
Spanish: CROACK!
Swedish: KOUACK!

Geese
German: SCHNATTER-SCHNATTER!
Japanese: BOO BOO!

Owls
Japanese: HO-HO!
Russian: OOKH!

Pigs
French: GROIN GROIN!
German: GRUNZ!
Russian: KROO!

Roosters
Japanese: KO-KI-KOKO!
Russian: KU-KA-RZHI-KU!

Tweety-birds
Chinese: CHU-CHU!
French: KWI-KWI!

Cats
Spanish, Portuguese, and
German: MIAU!

```
                        M F O
                      S R I G G
                      C R O A C K E
                      H H G R U
                      N A M       A
                      A V N
                      T H U
                    W T A U
K R O O S         I O T E V U
H I O N I O R G N I O R G H S
  K B I W K I W K N O S T U A D
  K O K I K O K O U A C K H U C
    O O V N H A U G N H A U G K
    B B U A T O G R U N Z H A F
    R O G U K I H Z R A K U K
      T H H A V T O G T O H
      E C S Q A U A T K
        U             E
        H             R Q U
        C A K
```

11. FALL IN LINE

The grid contains words associated with the fall season. The hidden message gives two names given in Great Britain for what Americans call Indian Summer, a time when fall weather is much warmer than usual.

```
O  S  R  O  L  O  C  E  E  R  T
L  R  A  K  I  N  G  Q  D  W  H
R  E  D  I  C  N  M  U  T  U  A
I  B  P  U  M  P  K  I  N  S  N
C  M  V  E  S  S  N  W  U  K
R  E  S  E  T  C  L  O  C  K  S
O  V  M  L  M  E  H  X  C  R  G
P  O  O  E  R  S  A  O  O  A  I
S  N  C  C  V  L  L  L  O  H  V
F  O  O  T  B  A  L  L  L  L  I
A  L  W  I  O  L  O  O  E  W  N
N  E  S  O  U  B  W  M  R  M  G
N  E  R  N  T  S  E  V  R  A  H
W  O  R  L  D  S  E  R  I  E  S
V  E  T  E  R  A  N  S  D  A  Y
```

AUTUMN	NOVEMBER
CIDER	OCTOBER
COOLER	PUMPKINS
CROPS	RAKING
ELECTION	RESET CLOCKS
EQUINOX	SCHOOL
FOOTBALL	THANKSGIVING
HALLOWEEN	TREE COLORS
HARVEST	VETERANS DAY
NEW TV SHOWS	WORLD SERIES

12. BE A GOOD SPORT

Shaped like a football helmet, the grid contains the names of different kinds of sports equipment. The hidden message tells you how you can use a piece of baseball equipment in your house.

```
            H  M  J  U  S  S  T
         O  D  R  A  O  B  K  C  A  B
      O  S  N  O  R  I  G  I  I  S  E  L
   P  G  O  L  F  B  A  G  L  K  S  T  L
   R  U  N  N  I  N  G  S  H  O  E  S  A  A
   T  O  T  F  N  F  O  D  F  Y  V  O  B  B
         T  U  K  U  R  A  C  K  E  T  A
         E  R  C  A        H  I  O  S
         R  O  U        U  S  O  E
            M  G  P  S  E  K  F  S
            N  M  G  O  A  L  P
H  O  C  K  E  Y  S  T  I  C  K  E  T  T
L                 A  W  H  E  L  M  E  T
G  O  G  G  L  E  S     S  O  T  E  S
                  P  E  S
```

BACKBOARD	IRONS
BASES	POLE
BATS	PUCK
BIKE	PUTTER
FOOTBALL	RACKET
GLOVE	RUNNING SHOES
GOAL	SHIN GUARDS
GOGGLES	SKATES
GOLF BAG	SKIS
HELMET	SWIMSUIT
HOCKEY STICK	TEES
HOOP	UNIFORM

13. ANIMATED MOVIES

The grid contains the names of 20 popular animated movies, some hand-drawn and others computer-animated. The hidden message runs together the titles of two animated Disney classics to make the name of a movie we'd like to see.

```
E  L  A  T  K  R  A  H  S  A  S
L  I  I  B  M  A  B  E  N  E  P
I  T  H  C  N  C  G  T  U  A  I
Y  T  E  B  E  S  Z  P  R  I  R
R  L  R  S  R  A  C  E  N  S  O
O  E  C  E  A  G  G  T  E  A  N
T  M  U  O  L  A  U  E  K  T  G
S  E  L  B  I  D  E  R  C  N  I
Y  R  E  M  O  A  T  P  I  A  A
O  M  S  U  N  M  D  A  H  F  N
T  A  Y  D  K  L  A  N  C  K  T
F  I  N  D  I  N  G  N  E  M  O
N  D  D  W  N  A  Z  R  A  T  T
H  D  E  L  G  O  H  E  B  E  A
S  A  B  U  G  S  L  I  F  E  T
```

A BUG'S LIFE	[THE] INCREDIBLES
ANTZ	IRON GIANT
BAMBI	[THE] LION KING
CARS	[THE] LITTLE MERMAID
CHICKEN RUN	MADAGASCAR
DELGO	PETER PAN
DUMBO	SHARK TALE
FANTASIA	SHREK
FINDING NEMO	TARZAN
HERCULES	TOY STORY
ICE AGE	[THE] WILD

14. DO YOU FOLLOW ME?

The grid contains things you follow. The hidden message defines good leaders.

```
T  O  U  R  G  U  I  D  E  T  H
S  U  I  T  E  Y  L  A  P  D  D
N  O  R  R  O  E  D  O  I  U  W
O  C  R  A  A  E  M  R  G  O  O
I  R  E  D  L  D  E  K  E  I  R
T  A  E  I  E  C  V  C  D  E  C
C  R  E  T  T  R  R  I  D  C  S
U  S  S  I  G  N  S  R  C  N  T
R  N  O  O  O  U  E  B  T  E  C
T  N  M  N  S  A  O  W  R  I  N
S  H  E  P  M  F  Y  O  O  C  I
N  L  E  X  A  M  P  L  E  S  T
I  C  L  A  E  T  O  L  W  N  S
T  W  E  N  R  R  H  E  S  O  N
I  D  E  A  L  T  N  Y  S  C  I
```

ADVICE

[YOUR] CONSCIENCE

[THE] CROWD

DIRECTIONS

[YOUR] DREAM

[THE] ENEMY

[AN] EXAMPLE

[YOUR] HEART

[AN] IDEAL

[YOUR] INSTINCTS

INSTRUCTIONS

[THE] LEADER

[THE] LOGIC

[THE] NEWS

[YOUR] NOSE

ORDERS

[THE] PATH

[THE] SIGNS

SUIT

[A] SUSPECT

[A] TOUR GUIDE

TRADITION

[THE] YELLOW BRICK ROAD

15. IN A PET STORE

Shaped like a doghouse, the grid contains supplies found in a pet store. The hidden message tells you what official sportswear you can now buy for your favorite pooch.

```
                    H
                  A S M
                E T A R C
              L I T T E R B O X
            T W E S N L S E T A G
        N T S O P G N I H C T A R C S
          D F B Y R A L L O C L E L
          O O R S S T C C A T N I P
          G R E R R R E D E E F R F
          T P T E N         R T B R I
          A E A P           I A A S
          G T W P           U B C H
          S F D I           C R O T
          G O J L           S U E A
          R O S C           I S E N
          S D E B           B H Y K
```

BEDS	FILTER
BIRDCAGE	FISH TANK
BISCUIT	GATES
BRUSH	LEASH
CARRIER	LITTER BOX
CATNIP	MATS
CLIPPERS	PET FOOD
COLLAR	SCRATCHING POST
CRATE	TOYS
DOG TAGS	TREATS
FEEDER	WATER BOWL

16. STAR SEARCH

Every item in the word list contains the letters S-T-A-R in consecutive order. When these letters appear in the star-shaped grid, they have been replaced by a ★. So, for example, OFF TO A RUNNING START would appear as OFFTOARUNNING★T. The hidden message is a sentence in which you'll also be SEEING ★S.

```
                        T
                    T   S   H
                    ★   E   E
                L   E   S   I   F
                L   ★   S   ★   P   I   D
    K   ★   S   P   A   N   G   L   E   D   B   A   N   N   E   R   Y
    E   Z   A   G   ★   N   A   I   ★   V   M   E   L   ★   H
        R   G   E   N   I   F   V   U   E   G   O   R   C
            T   S   E   T   N   O   C   G   N   I   ★
                ★   A   O   C   M   T   E   I   M
                L   R   O   W   ★   ★   U   V   ★
            A   T   ★   H   H   S   S   P   A   V   T
            H   I   E   S   T       H   ★   R   E   E
        ★   C   A   E   A           T   K   D   B   M
        A   D   R   T               ★   R   E   U
    ★   ★   F   E                       O   A   ★   U
    T   N                                   D   D
```

ALL-STARS	MUSTARD
COSTA RICA	NORTH STAR
CUSTARD PIE	SHOOTING STAR
DARK STAR	STAR TREK
FALSE START	STARCHY
FRESH START	STARGAZE
HEADSTART	STARING CONTEST
"I'M STARVED!"	STARK-RAVING MAD
LONE STAR STATE	STAR-SPANGLED BANNER
MOVIE STARS	UPSTART

17. FROM A TO Z

The grid below contains 26 words that we think are fun to say and hear. For variety, each word starts with a different letter of the alphabet. The hidden message is a pangram, which is a sentence or phrase, often non-sensical, that contains all 26 letters of the alphabet.

```
K  U  Y  D  E  G  G  A  R  P  W
A  A  T  T  O  B  O  G  G  A  N
A  T  Z  H  E  P  Z  N  N  O  U
L  A  N  O  G  A  I  D  H  O  N
O  A  K  R  O  K  O  V  O  W  I
D  S  K  C  I  T  S  P  O  H  C
N  I  R  V  I  Q  N  R  R  F  O
O  G  A  O  U  R  B  I  A  U  R
G  X  V  I  W  E  E  S  Y  Z  N
O  D  D  L  Y  A  L  M  S  Z  Q
U  I  R  E  X  C  K  Z  I  Y  B
Q  U  A  R  T  E  T  G  Z  L  J
L  Y  A  F  E  D  Z  B  O  O  I
O  Y  O  Y  U  A  G  G  J  A  N
S  M  M  E  G  A  B  Y  T  E  X
```

AARDVARK	NOZZLE
BLOG	ODDLY
CHOPSTICKS	PRISM
DIAGONAL	QUARTET
EYEBROW	RAGGEDY
FUZZY	SQUID
GONDOLA	TOBOGGAN
HOORAY	UNICORN
IPOD	VIKING
JINX	WAND
KAZOO	X-RAYS
LIMERICK	YO-YO
MEGABYTE	ZIGZAG

18. ACHOO!

The grid contains words associated with sneezing. The hidden message is a curious fact about what happens to people when they sneeze.

```
M  G  A  L  D  A  N  D  E  R  M
C  O  M  M  O  N  C  O  L  D  S
R  D  L  O  S  T  O  H  S  E  P
I  B  V  D  E  R  V  Y  O  E  R
A  L  R  E  P  P  E  P  H  O  E
F  E  U  B  S  O  R  A  N  E  A
O  S  D  F  N  Y  Y  C  E  L  D
T  S  U  D  E  F  O  L  L  K  G
S  Y  O  S  E  C  U  E  L  C  E
R  O  E  V  Z  S  R  T  O  I  R
U  U  E  H  E  G  M  O  P  T  M
B  R  E  I  Y  R  O  E  F  Y  S
T  I  E  H  D  N  U  S  E  G  E
S  N  O  I  T  A  T  I  R  R  I
T  H  G  I  L  T  H  G  I  R  B
```

"ACHOO!"	"GOD BLESS YOU"
ALLERGY	HAY FEVER
BRIGHT LIGHT	IRRITATION
BURST OF AIR	MOLD
COMMON COLD	NOSE
"COVER YOUR MOUTH!"	PEPPER
DANDER	POLLEN
DUST	SNEEZE
FORCEFUL	SPREAD GERMS
"GESUNDHEIT!"	TICKLE

19. WHAT I GO THROUGH

The grid and the hidden message contain things people go through.

```
C  T  I  H  L  E  F  G  M  O  T
R  G  N  I  N  I  A  R  T  S  Y
I  I  S  O  L  T  M  N  M  E  C
S  T  P  E  E  S  E  O  D  C  T
I  L  E  N  N  U  T  A  R  R  P
S  C  C  H  P  S  A  A  A  E  U
T  D  T  A  U  N  L  P  W  T  R
E  G  I  C  F  E  D  U  E  P  K
K  N  O  V  O  O  E  R  R  A  N
C  E  N  T  O  H  T  S  S  S  A
O  E  Z  R  D  R  E  E  R  S  B
P  A  N  A  M  A  C  A  N  A  L
Y  E  N  O  M  O  T  E  O  G  I
T  O  L  L  B  O  O  T  H  E  F
E  L  I  T  S  N  R  U  T  F  E
```

BANKRUPTCY	METAL DETECTOR
CRISIS	MONEY
CUSTOMS	PAIN
DIVORCE	PANAMA CANAL
DRAWERS	POCKETS
FILE	PURSE
FOOD	SECRET PASSAGE
GATE	TOLLBOOTH
INSPECTION	TRAINING
LIFE	TRAPDOOR
LIST	TUNNEL
MAZE	TURNSTILE

20. JUST BEAT IT

Shaped like a kettledrum, the grid contains the names of different drums and percussion instruments. The hidden message answers this riddle: Why did the competitive girl prefer to play her drum than play her brother in video games?

```
      B  E  C  T  A  M  B  O  U  R  I  N  E
   T  U  B  U  L  A  R  B  E  L  L  S  C  A  K
   C  U  S  E  R  S  X  Y  L  O  P  H  O  N  E
   A  H  E  I  C  W  N  O  L  L  I  R  A  C  T
   S  R  M  O  U  O  L  D  G  M  S  A  L  W  T
   T  B  A  G  L  O  C  K  E  N  S  P  I  E  L
   A     A  T  Y  D  S  S  A  B  O  G  E     E
   N        A  T  B  T  R  T  T  N  B        D
   E           L  L  E  B  W  O  C           R
   T              O  E  H  G  M              U
   S              C        T                 M
      E           K        O           A
         V        E        M        R
            A        D     R     A
               L     U     M     C
               C  O  N  G  A
               T  R  A  P  S  E  T
```

BONGO
CARILLON
CASTANETS
CHIMES
CLAVES
CONGA
COWBELL
GLOCKENSPIEL
GONG
KETTLEDRUM

MARACAS
MARIMBA
RATTLE
SNARE
TAMBOURINE
TOM-TOM
TRAP SET
TUBULAR BELLS
WOODBLOCK
XYLOPHONE

21. OPEN UP!

The grid contains things you open. The hidden message contains two things you can open without using your hands.

```
G  C  A  N  O  F  S  O  U  P  E
A  A  E  S  A  C  T  I  U  S  W
H  N  R  Z  I  P  P  E  R  I  C
T  D  C  A  R  T  R  U  N  K  G
U  Y  O  N  G  V  P  D  E  I  R
O  W  C  R  E  E  O  S  F  A  E
M  R  T  R  F  W  D  T  B  I  E
B  A  N  K  A  C  C  O  U  N  T
O  P  I  L  S  T  T  N  O  A  I
R  P  L  L  L  T  E  N  F  R  N
J  E  W  E  L  R  Y  B  O  X  G
T  R  K  E  A  D  U  S  L  Y  C
O  U  O  C  W  R  E  N  D  M  A
I  N  O  D  O  Y  S  T  E  R  R
U  M  B  R  E  L  L  A  R  M  D
```

BANK ACCOUNT	LOCKER
BOOK	MAIL
BOTTLE	MENU
CAN OF SOUP	[YOUR] MOUTH
CANDY WRAPPER	OYSTER
CAR TRUNK	PURSE
CRATE	SUITCASE
[YOUR] EYES	UMBRELLA
FOLDER	WALL SAFE
GARAGE DOOR	WALLET
GIFT	WINDOW
GREETING CARD	ZIPPER
JEWELRY BOX	

22. WORKING LATE

The grid contains the occupations of people who work at night. The hidden message asks a question about these workers at the end of their night shifts.

```
D  S  U  A  L  C  A  T  N  A  S
O  R  T  A  H  D  T  E  I  C  Y
S  S  O  S  T  I  O  L  G  L  L
R  P  S  T  A  Y  L  C  H  U  L
E  C  R  R  I  E  I  T  T  B  F
V  A  N  O  S  N  P  C  W  O  I
I  T  E  N  G  A  A  A  W  R
R  B  W  O  L  R  I  J  T  N  E
D  U  S  M  L  T  A  I  C  E  M
S  R  M  E  E  T  A  M  H  R  E
U  G  A  R  B  A  G  E  M  A  N
B  L  N  C  A  B  B  Y  A  E  U
D  A  A  J  U  D  G  E  N  Y  R
K  R  E  L  C  L  E  T  O  H  S
T  O  O  T  H  F  A  I  R  Y  E
```

ASTRONOMER	JANITOR
BUS DRIVERS	[NIGHT COURT] JUDGE
CABBY	NEWSMAN
CAT BURGLAR	NIGHT WATCHMAN
CLUB OWNER	NURSE
DOCTOR	PILOT
DRACULA	PROGRAMMER
FIREMEN	SANTA CLAUS
GARBAGEMAN	TOOTH FAIRY
HOTEL CLERK	WAITER

23. RING-A-DING-DING

Shaped like a big engagement ring, the grid and the hidden message contain things with rings.

```
O L Y M P I C F L A G P H
A R C H E R Y T A R G E T
  A N O R O C P O P E O
    D A R T B O A R D
      N E R M E L E
      G E I       L L N
    B R D         L A F
    T E           V R
    S N           E O
    A A           L D
    T D T         H S O
      E T U     U B L
        C I R C U S A
          K I N G H
```

ARCHERY TARGET
BELL
BRIDE
CIRCUS
COLLAR
CORONA
DARTBOARD
FRODO
GRENADE

GROOM
HALO
KING
NAVELS
OLYMPIC FLAG
POPE
SATURN
TREE

24. ALL TOGETHER NOW

Each of the 10 words on the list below is commonly paired with another word. For example, TABLE goes with CHAIR—which is the shape of the grid. To begin, figure out the second word in each pair by filling in the blanks. (We give you the first letter in each missing word. If you need more help, the full list is on page 66.) Then find all 20 words in the grid.

One more thing…the words "united" and "together" are synonyms of one another. The hidden message tells you where many of us would be living if things had been a little different.

```
      S   E   I   R   F   I   D   N   T
      R   T   L   H   E   T   O   O   S
      A   I   G   B   U   R   G   E   R
      L   R   E   R   A   T   S   G   A
      L   W   E   C   A   T   S   N   T
      O   A   H   H   R   E   C   I   S
      D   R   O   I   S   T   A   H   T
      E   S   P   S   K   C   O   S   A
      E   E   I   O   F   E   A   I   H   I
      S   M   N   S   S   E   R   W   I   I   R
      I       G   E   N   T   L   E   M   E   N   C
      R       I               C               E
              D               A               N
              A                               T
              L                               S
```

1. BURGER and F __ __ __ __
2. CATS and D __ __ __
3. DOLLARS and C __ __ __ __
4. LADIES and G __ __ __ __ __ __ __ __
5. READ and W __ __ __ __
6. RISE and S __ __ __ __
7. SOCKS and S __ __ __ __
8. STARS and S __ __ __ __ __ __
9. TABLE and C __ __ __ __
10. WISHING and H __ __ __ __ __

25. A WORK OF ART

The grid contains things you use to make art, and the hidden message tells what the most important thing to use is.

```
I  T  F  A  B  R  I  C  R  S  T
G  L  I  T  T  E  R  N  E  S  A
R  E  N  A  E  L  C  E  P  I  P
O  U  G  T  T  H  C  E  A  R  E
M  L  E  S  T  A  M  P  P  A  D
K  G  R  A  N  S  Y  W  N  P  T
B  L  P  V  E  R  A  R  O  F  I
U  P  A  S  T  E  L  S  I  O  S
T  S  I  H  A  K  C  T  T  R  D
T  K  N  L  C  R  S  I  C  E  A
O  N  T  E  A  A  I  C  U  T  E
N  I  T  Y  P  M  S  K  R  S  B
S  R  O  L  O  C  R  E  T  A  W
T  N  H  E  L  I  I  R  S  L  O
S  T  R  I  N  G  M  S  N  P  I
A  G  O  C  H  A  R  C  O  A  L
I  F  N  A  T  M  I  O  C  N  S
```

BEADS	INKS
BUTTONS	MAGIC MARKERS
CANVAS	OILS
CHALK	PASTELS
CHARCOAL	PENS
CLAY	PIPE CLEANER
CONSTRUCTION PAPER	PLASTER OF PARIS
CRAYONS	STAMP PAD
FABRIC	STICKERS
FINGERPAINT	STRING
FOIL	TAPE
GLITTER	WATERCOLORS
GLUE	WOOD

26. GLASS

Shaped like a perfume bottle, the grid contains things that are always or sometimes made of glass. The hidden message poses a question about an 8-ounce glass that has 4 ounces of liquid in it.

```
          T  I  S
          N  I  L
       B  E  A  D  S
          M  S  T
       P  A  H  A  A
       S  N  E  L  V
    P  A  P  E  R  W  E  I  G  H  T
 E  N  A  P  W  O  D  N  I  W  L  U  F
 C  W  I  N  D  S  H  I  E  L  D  B  F
 U  U  L  C  H  A  N  D  E  L  I  E  R
 P  E  R  F  U  M  E  B  O  T  T  L  E
 S  E  L  B  A  T  E  E  F  F  O  C  L
 O  R  C  R  Y  S  T  A  L  B  A  L  L
 A  Q  U  A  R  I  U  M  S  I  R  P  H
    R  O  O  D  R  E  W  O  H  S  A
    J  L  I  G  H  T  B  U  L  B  S
       A  W  L  C  F  E  M  P  G
       R  O  R  R  I  M  U
       S  B  T  Y  J
```

AQUARIUM	LENS
BEADS	LIGHT BULBS
BOWL	MIRROR
CHANDELIER	PAPERWEIGHT
CHRISTMAS ORNAMENT	PERFUME BOTTLE
COFFEE TABLE	PRISM
CRYSTAL BALL	SHOWER DOOR
CUPS	TUBE
JARS	VASE
JUGS	WINDOWPANE
LAMP	WINDSHIELD

27. SIGNS AHEAD

Shaped like a stop sign, the grid contains wording on road signs commonly seen in the U.S. The hidden message is NOT one you'll ever see on a road sign, but it would be a huge help if it were put in the right places.

```
            D  U  M  D  L
         M  M  D  L  E  Y  E
      L  Y  E  E  O  R  K  N  U
   P  L  T  I  N  Y  N  U  O  J  F
N  M  O  Y  T  U  A  O  S  Z  O  T  Y
O  U  T  M  F  E  W  T  I  L  S  L  W
R  B  Y  S  E  X  E  H  W  O  N  E  E
T  F  A  L  L  I  N  G  R  O  C  K  S
H  S  P  D  E  T  O  I  S  H  R  Y  T
   Y  A  W  G  N  O  R  W  C  O  K
      U  E  R  R  A  O  O  S  E
         X  E  C  I  N  L  T
            M  P  O  T  S
```

BUMP	NO RIGHT ON RED
CARS ONLY	NORTH
DETOUR	ONE-WAY
EAST	PAY TOLL
EXIT	SCHOOL ZONE
FALLING ROCKS	SLOW
FUEL	STOP
LOOK	WEST
MEN AT WORK	WRONG WAY
MERGE LEFT	YIELD

28. LOST IN CYBERSPACE

Shaped like a computer screen, the grid contains words and phrases connected to the Internet. The hidden message answers this riddle: What do virtual online astronauts live in?

```
P O A B E W E D I W D L R O W
H I N S T A N T M E S S A G E
I S G L S N I G U L P Y P M C
S E G O I Y G B S N O Z A M A
H T O E L N N R K R C I S B S
I I O O P B E A R H L C S E E
N R G O S K H D A O L N W O D
G O L H C L C T M S B L O C K
N V E A S P R A K R V I R U S
C A H Y E P A U O S M E D O M
T F A H O M E W O R K H E L P
            S E B
          E T I D O
      S C R E E N N A M E N
```

AMAZON	INSTANT MESSAGE
BLOCK	LOG ON
BLOG	MODEM
BOOKMARK	ONLINE
BROWSER	PASSWORD
CHAT	PHISHING
DOWNLOAD	PLUG-INS
EBAY	SCREEN NAME
E-MAIL	SEARCH ENGINE
FAVORITES	URLS
GOOGLE	VIRUS
HACKERS	WORLD WIDE WEB
HIGH-SPEED	YAHOO
HOMEWORK HELP	

29. PLAYING PINBALL

The grid contains words and phrases associated with pinball. The hidden message tells where you can play more than 150 different pinball machines in one location.

```
S  H  O  O  T  A  G  A  I  N  P
P  T  I  B  R  E  N  N  I  P  S
R  N  L  L  A  B  R  A  L  L  U
I  F  L  I  P  P  E  R  S  L  N
N  Q  H  N  T  A  P  P  L  L  O
G  U  L  K  C  O  L  L  L  A  B
H  A  F  I  O  U  A  F  F  B  A
I  R  R  N  N  M  Y  E  S  A  A
G  T  E  G  R  A  T  P  O  R  D
H  E  E  L  B  U  M  P  C  T  N
S  R  G  I  S  A  T  A  L  X  E
C  S  A  G  R  H  D  R  A  E  K
O  S  M  H  V  E  A  E  U  G  O
R  A  E  T  J  A  C  K  P  O  T
E  V  A  S  P  A  L  S  E  S  Y
```

ARCADE	QUARTERS
BALL LOCK	RAMPS
BLINKING LIGHTS	REPLAY
BONUS	SHAKE
BUMP	SHOOT AGAIN
DROP TARGET	SLAP SAVE
EXTRA BALL	SPINNER
FLIPPERS	SPRING
FREE GAME	TILT
HIGH SCORE	TOKEN
JACKPOT	TRAP
PLUNGER	"YOUR TURN!"

30. TOP-OF-THE-LINE

Every item in the word list contains the letters T-O-P in consecutive order. When these letters appear in the spinning-top-shaped grid, they have been replaced by a ♠. So, for example, TOPEKA, KANSAS would appear as ♠EKAKANSAS. The hidden message tells what you might do if you get really frustrated with this puzzle.

AUTOPILOT	ISOTOPE	TOP DOG
BACKSTOP	LAPTOP	TOP HAT
BUS STOP	NONSTOP	TOP TEN
CHRISTOPHER	OCTOPUS	TOPICS
COLUMBUS	ON TOP OF	TOPSOIL
COME TO PASS	PUT A STOP TO	TOPSPIN
FLATTOP	ROOFTOP	TOPSY-TURVY
FROM TOP TO	STOP BY	TRICERATOPS
BOTTOM	STOPLIGHTS	UTOPIA

31. IT'S ABOUT TIME

The grid contains words about periods of time. The hidden message contains two definitions of one of these words other than its time meaning. Can you figure out which word it is?

```
A  T  N  O  O  N  R  E  T  F  A
D  A  Y  T  I  M  E  V  Y  Y  S
O  I  N  O  G  A  S  E  C  R  U
L  M  I  L  L  E  N  N  I  U  M
E  G  A  E  L  D  D  I  M  T  M
S  M  K  O  A  A  A  N  W  N  E
C  O  I  S  F  C  W  G  E  E  R
E  N  R  T  U  E  N  E  E  C  E
N  T  O  R  T  D  U  M  K  N  T
C  H  I  L  D  H  O  O  D  D  N
E  O  I  N  G  R  G  C  A  R  I
S  E  C  O  N  D  Y  I  Y  H  W
O  O  M  I  N  U  T  E  N  O  K
E  D  N  E  K  E  E  W  A  U  D
N  G  N  I  R  P  S  E  S  R  S
```

ADOLESCENCE	MINUTE
AFTERNOON	MONTH
CENTURY	MORNING
CHILDHOOD	NIGHTTIME
DAWN	OLD AGE
DAYTIME	SECOND
DECADE	SPRING
DUSK	SUMMER
EVENING	WEEKDAY
FALL	WEEKEND
HOUR	WINTER
MIDDLE AGE	YEAR
MILLENNIUM	

32. MAPS, DNA, AND SPAM

The grid contains 20 palindromes: words or phrases that read the same either forwards or backwards. The hidden message is a long and funny palindrome. The grid is shaped like a cartoon detonator box of TNT (a three-letter palindrome). And if you were wondering about the puzzle's title…well, it's a palindrome, too.

```
      G O T U N A N U T
            E
            V
            E
            R
  B O R R O W O R R O B I S
  H A N G O L D L O G G D T
  N I F I H A D A H I F I A
  U K L I O N O I L P A D C
  R A C E C A R L A U S D K
  S Y A W E F E W T F L I C
  E A T A M G V I O F P D A
  S K I A G M E A Y U E I T
  R S T E P O N N O P E T S
  U L L A S P A G T N P A H
  N Y O B A N A N A B O Y O
  A S A N T A A T N A S A G
```

A SANTA AT NASA	NURSES RUN
A TOYOTA	PEEP
BORROW OR ROB	PUFF UP
GOLD LOG	RACECAR
I DID, DID I?	STACK CATS
IF I HAD A HI-FI	STEP ON NO PETS
KAYAK	TAP PAT
LEG GEL	TUNA NUT
LION OIL	WE FEW
NEVER ODD OR EVEN	YO! BANANA BOY!

33. TAKE A WALK

The grid and the hidden message contain things people walk on.

```
B  A  L  A  N  C  E  B  E  A  M
R  O  O  L  F  H  C  A  E  B  A
O  S  L  L  E  H  S  G  G  E  M
K  L  T  H  O  U  N  N  D  C  K
E  A  T  I  P  T  O  E  I  R  L
N  O  T  L  G  O  A  T  R  U  A
E  C  I  L  M  H  Y  E  B  N  W
S  T  A  G  E  S  T  P  T  W  E
C  O  U  N  T  R  Y  R  O  A  D
A  H  G  R  A  S  S  A  O  Y  I
L  N  E  A  R  T  H  C  F  P  S
A  E  T  R  H  A  N  D  S  A  E
T  L  L  I  M  D  A  E  R  T  I
O  L  K  L  A  W  D  R  A  O  B
R  U  O  F  L  L  A  B  R  U  C
```

BALANCE BEAM	GRASS
BALL FOUR	HANDS
BEACH	HILL
BOARDWALK	HOT COALS
BROKEN ESCALATOR	MOON
CITY STREET	RED CARPET
COUNTRY ROAD	RUNWAY
CURB	SIDEWALK
EARTH	STAGE
EGGSHELLS	TIGHTROPE
FLOOR	TIPTOE
FOOTBRIDGE	TREADMILL

34. SOUNDS FAMILIAR

The flower-shaped grid contains 15 pairs of homophones: words that sound alike but are spelled differently, like FLOWER and FLOUR. The hidden message uses two more pairs of homophones in a sentence.

```
      F  F            A  E            P  B
      L  L  P      R  T  B  O      P  E  L
      E  O  O      I  O  W  G      D  A  U
      E  W  H  U  W  E  R  E  I  R  C  E
      G  E  S  L  R  E  T  S  R  A  E  N
         R  E  N  A  V  G  O  N  H  D
         D  E  S  S  U  C  S  I  D  T
         E  E  S  C  O  K  E  S
   A           T  C  G  A  M  V           D
   T  W        A  E  X  I           D  L
   E  E  J        N  O           C  M  O
   F  L  E  A     E  V        A  R  V  B
      B  A  W     S  E        D  E  E
      A  N  R  S  I  R     P  R  W  R
      S  O  O  U  D     D  F  S
         I  T  H  R  O  U  G  H
         T  E  C  E  I  P
```

BLEW	BLUE
BOLD	BOWLED
CHORALE	CORRAL
COAX	COKES
CREWS	CRUISE
DISCUSSED	DISGUST
FLEA	FLEE
FLOUR	FLOWER
GENES	JEANS
GREASE	GREECE
OVERDO	OVERDUE
PEACE	PIECE
SUITE	SWEET
THREW	THROUGH
VANE	VEIN

35. FOR GOOD MEASURE

The grid contains the names of units of measurement for a lot of different kinds of things—like distance, weight, and time. The hidden message mentions three things that a degree is used for in measuring.

```
T  L  E  R  R  A  B  E  M  P  C
N  E  E  R  A  G  T  G  U  R  A
M  A  R  G  I  T  N  E  C  C  R
A  G  N  L  O  O  A  E  R  B  A
R  U  L  O  L  L  U  E  A  U  T
D  E  F  R  S  T  T  N  K  S  Y
S  Q  U  A  R  E  I  N  C  H  A
I  F  T  U  M  D  C  E  E  E  R
D  N  U  O  P  F  A  O  P  L  D
A  N  L  G  A  L  L  O  N  D  E
P  I  N  T  L  O  M  N  Q  D  C
K  G  H  I  T  T  I  B  U  C  I
N  O  O  P  S  E  L  B  A  T  B
M  U  H  A  N  D  E  G  R  E  E
D  N  O  O  P  S  A  E  T  E  L
```

ACRE	HAND
BARREL	KILOMETER
BUSHEL	LEAGUE
CARAT	NANOSECOND
CENTIGRAM	NAUTICAL MILE
CUBIT	OUNCE
DECIBEL	PECK
DEGREE	PINT
DRAM	POUND
FATHOM	QUART
FOOT	SQUARE INCH
FURLONG	TABLESPOON
GALLON	TEASPOON
GILL	YARD

36. ALL AROUND AFRICA

The grid contains the names of 24 countries in Africa, the continent with the largest number of countries—more than 50. The hidden message mentions the four African countries whose names contain the letter Z.

```
S  I  E  R  R  A  L  E  O  N  E
O  A  L  O  G  N  A  I  O  M  O
U  T  A  H  Z  A  T  O  B  M  B
T  U  A  I  I  Q  R  P  U  Y  L
H  N  E  T  L  E  A  O  Y  U  A
A  I  B  I  M  A  N  H  B  G  G
F  S  V  A  A  N  M  T  O  A  E
R  I  C  O  U  O  G  O  T  N  N
I  A  Z  A  R  N  N  S  S  D  E
C  H  A  D  I  Y  U  E  W  A  S
A  B  I  G  T  D  C  L  A  A  Z
A  M  E  B  A  I  A  O  N  Z  I
M  R  B  N  N  A  D  N  A  W  R
B  U  R  K  I  N  A  F  A  S  O
K  E  N  Y  A  N  A  B  W  E  T
```

ANGOLA	MAURITANIA
BENIN	NAMIBIA
BOTSWANA	NIGER
BURKINA FASO	RWANDA
CAMEROON	SENEGAL
CHAD	SIERRA LEONE
EGYPT	SOMALIA
GHANA	SOUTH AFRICA
IVORY COAST	SUDAN
KENYA	TOGO
LESOTHO	TUNISIA
LIBYA	UGANDA

37. WHAT'S THAT IN THE SKY?

You may recognize the Big Dipper in the night sky, but this grid contains the names of 18 lesser-known constellations such as the Arrow, which is the shape of the grid. The hidden message names three more constellations that may surprise you.

```
        S  Q  U  A  R  E  R
        C  P  E  I  E  S  O
        H  O  V  A  L  C  T
        A  E  M  I  G  O  P
        R  C  A  P  N  K  L
        E  S  G  D  A  O  U
        E  L  P  I  I  S  C
        T  N  E  P  R  E  S
        O  H  L  I  T  A  N
        I  Y  A  W  O  L  F
  M  I  C  R  O  S  C  O  P  E  F  N  D
     N  E  A  I  R  P  U  M  P  W  E
        A  H  S  I  F  D  L  O  G
        C  R  A  N  E  R  T
        U  A  B  R  L
        O  A  E
        T
```

AIR PUMP	MICROSCOPE
ARROW	RIVER
CHARIOTEER	SAILS
COMPASS	SCULPTOR
CRANE	SERPENT
GIRAFFE	SQUARE
GOLDFISH	TOUCAN
HARE	TRIANGLE
LYRE	WOLF

38. SEUSS IN USE

Shaped like the hat in *The Cat in the Hat*, the grid contains words found in the books of Dr. Seuss. The hidden message is a fun fact about *Green Eggs and Ham*.

```
            T  M  A  I  M  A  S
         R  B  H  E  M  A  Y  O  R
      S  N  E  E  T  C  H  E  S  W
      K  H  F  D  U  O  D  R  L
      C  E  T  B  F  B  N  T
      O  O  B  O  K  I  A  L
      S  I  H  Z  H  U  S  E
   S  N  E  S  O  O  J  G  H
   S  I  N  R  U  P  W  G  S  1
   Y  X  T  W  T  H  O  E  G  F
   I  O  I  F  O  O  T  N  R  Y
   N  F  D  V  B  R  I  E  P  L
   K  I  I  L  F  H  B  E  F  O
   E  L  E  R  T  E  N  R  T  R  P
   L  C  H  C  N  I  R  G  M  A  W
O  E  K  R              X  O  R  G
D                                S
```

BEFT	MR. BROWN
CUBBINS	OOBLECK
FOX IN SOCKS	RED FISH
"GREEN EGGS AND HAM"	SAM I AM
GRINCH	SNEETCHES
GROX	THING 1
"HOP ON POP"	WHO-VILLE
HORTON	YERTLE
LORAX	YINK
MAYOR	ZOWER

39. WORD CHAIN

The words in this puzzle form a chain in which the letter that ends one word is the same letter that begins the next word. For example, if the first word were THROW, the next word would begin with a W. And if that next word were WINTER, the word after that would begin with an R. Since the first and last letters of each word in the list are missing, it's up to you to figure out what the words are by filling in the blanks as you use the clues given.

If you get stuck, you can do three things: figure out a word and then work backward; search the grid below for the middle letters you already have and look for a letter on each end; or turn to page 66 for a full list of the words in the chain. The hidden message tells the difference between a chain and another common object.

```
U  S  N  F  L  G  A  L  A  X  Y
E  B  U  L  L  D  O  Z  E  R  E
I  G  S  O  L  V  I  N  G  I  L
N  K  G  G  I  E  A  M  C  H  L
V  R  L  S  G  T  Y  A  I  U  O
E  N  A  A  H  S  I  D  F  C  W
S  P  H  O  T  O  G  R  A  P  H
T  I  Y  E  N  I  E  U  T  R  C
I  L  R  A  I  D  P  M  E  U  T
G  Y  H  A  N  S  N  S  P  C  N
A  O  B  O  G  K  A  E  O  G  E
T  I  W  N  F  B  E  N  T  H  L
I  H  N  H  B  U  F  E  P  I  L
O  N  U  A  I  E  M  G  A  A  E
N  N  T  M  T  P  U  B  L  I  C
D  H  N  T  B  O  P  E  L  N  X
R  E  I  G  N  E  D  O  D  E  E
```

1. __ H O T O G R A P __   Picture in a magazine

2. __ O S P I T A __   Place where doctors and nurses work

3. __ I G H T N I N __   It can come with thunder

4. __ A L A X __   The Milky Way is the one we live in

5. __ E L L O __   Big Bird's color

6. __ O N D E R F U __   Terrific

7. __ A P T O __   Type of computer you can carry with you

8. __ U B L I __   Not private but open to everyone

9. __ O N F E T T __   Bits of paper you toss on New Year's Eve

10. __ N V E S T I G A T I O __   Part of TV's popular C.S.I.

11. __ U T R I T I O U __   Healthy, like food

12. __ A B B A T __   Holy day of the week for Jewish people

13. __ I P P __   Large, hoglike African river mammal, for short

14. __ G R __   Shrek is this kind of beast

15. __ X C E L L E N __   Very very good

16. __ H U M __   It's on a hand

17. __ U L L D O Z E __   Big earth-moving vehicle

18. __ E I G N E __   Ruled a country as the king

19. __ R U __   Instrument in a band

20. __ Y S T E R __   Something that can't be explained

21. __ A N K E __   New York baseball player

22. __ G G __   Things in an Easter basket

23. __ O L V I N __   Figuring out a puzzle or #20 above

24. __ O L __   Sport of Tiger Woods

25. __ U M B L __   Drop the football

40. THOSE WHO SERVE

The grid contains various military ranks in the United States and United Kingdom. It also contains the names of the four major branches of U.S. military service.

You may have heard of a 21-gun salute, which is given when a U.S. president arrives or departs. But there is an even bigger salute in the U.S. The hidden message tells you how big it is and when it is given.

```
L  A  R  O  P  R  O  C  A  F  N
I  S  E  R  G  E  A  N  T  A  S
F  T  R  Y  G  P  M  U  M  N  Q
L  I  E  U  T  E  N  A  N  T  U
A  S  C  A  S  A  E  L  J  U  A
H  E  I  E  N  S  I  G  N  O  D
S  N  F  T  E  O  N  E  P  J  R
R  I  F  G  E  N  E  R  A  L  O
A  R  O  L  U  L  I  O  Y  T  N
M  A  Y  N  A  V  Y  D  H  E  L
D  M  T  F  A  R  O  O  U  A  E
L  R  T  T  T  H  I  M  R  A  A
E  R  E  D  N  A  M  M  O  C  D
I  T  P  N  O  O  Y  O  D  N  E
F  A  I  R  F  O  R  C  E  A  R
```

ADMIRAL
AIR FORCE
ARMY
CAPTAIN
COMMANDER
COMMODORE
CORPORAL
ENSIGN
FIELD MARSHAL
GENERAL

LIEUTENANT
MAJOR
MARINES
NAVY
PETTY OFFICER
PRIVATE
SEAMAN
SERGEANT
SQUADRON LEADER

41. AT HOME PLATE

Shaped like a dinner plate, the grid contains many kinds of silverware that might be found next to a plate (or, in a few cases, in the kitchen) at a fancy restaurant. The word list is arranged by types of silverware, and the category titles KNIFE, FORK, and SPOON are also hidden in the grid. Although there is both a fish knife and fish fork, a dinner knife and dinner fork, plus a dessert knife, dessert fork, and dessert spoon, the words FISH, DINNER, and DESSERT appear only once each in the grid. The hidden message names two other pieces of silverware that are very common. Can you guess what they are before reading the message?

```
            S  O  U  P
         H  O  Y  W  A  B  H  O
      D  E  S  S  E  R  T  U  S  T
      A  T  B  S  A  S  T  K  U  I
   R  E  T  T  U  B  L  N  A  N  B  F
   R  F  E  L  E  T  I  A  S  D  P  C
   E  A  O  O  N  F  C  O  D  A  H  N
   K  E  S  N  E  P  I  H  L  E  U  F
      S  F  P  D  I  N  N  E  R  O
      A  T  F  O  U  G  S  E  R  A
      S  P  O  O  E  O  K  O
         W  C  N  N
```

KNIFE	FORK	SPOON
BUTCHER	DESSERT	COFFEE
BUTTER	DINNER	DESSERT
CHEESE	FISH	SUNDAE
DESSERT	FONDUE	SOUP
DINNER	OYSTER	WOODEN
FISH	SALAD	
SLICING		
STEAK		

42. THE IN CROWD

The words in the grid are parts of pairs. In the word list below, each item in the left column can be found in the pair item in the right column; for example, ACTRESS "in" MOVIE. The hidden message continues that theme.

```
Q U A R T E R B A C K
E D A C E D N O E A U
E I F F E L T O W E R
N W O L C G L K H T S
Y C O M T R E S E D S
A U T O M O B I L E E
H C B V I H T L S N R
C L A I D C A I I E T
N O L E M R E T A W C
C U L N A U S C H S A
I D G U E H A A H P P
R O A F M C S I R A P
C A M T T N V R O P U
U B E U L E S D E E S
S E S Y L I B R A R Y
```

ACTRESS	MOVIE
AISLE	CHURCH
BEES	HIVE
BOOKS	LIBRARY
CACTUS	DESERT
CLOWN	CIRCUS
COLUMN	NEWSPAPER
EIFFEL TOWER	PARIS
QUARTERBACK	FOOTBALL GAME
RAIN	CLOUD
SEAT BELT	AUTOMOBILE
SEEDS	WATERMELON
YEAR	DECADE

43. RHYME TIME

Every word given in the list below and in the hidden message ends with the sound of -ITE. The message names something you find on the front of a car.

```
S  N  A  K  E  B  I  T  E  R  T
T  P  L  A  Y  W  R  I  G  H  T
A  I  G  F  E  T  I  N  G  I  E
L  E  S  L  T  H  G  I  F  T  Y
A  X  H  A  P  P  E  T  I  T  E
C  C  T  S  T  H  T  K  H  P  S
T  I  E  H  N  E  R  H  A  F  I
I  T  E  L  G  M  L  R  T  Q  G
T  E  H  I  I  A  L  W  U  H
E  B  A  G  D  S  T  L  I  I  T
T  Y  H  H  I  I  L  N  L  T  G
I  T  E  T  I  N  U  I  I  E  E
V  E  E  T  I  L  O  P  G  K  H
N  E  T  I  M  R  E  T  H  H  S
I  T  D  Y  N  A  M  I  T  E  T
```

APPETITE	PARASITE
BYTE	PLAYWRIGHT
DYNAMITE	POLITE
EXCITE	QUITE
EYESIGHT	SATELLITE
FAHRENHEIT	SKINTIGHT
FIGHT	SLIGHT
FLASHLIGHT	SNAKEBITE
HEIGHT	STALACTITE
IGNITE	TERMITE
INVITE	TONIGHT
KITE	TWILIGHT
MIGHT	UNITE

44. CABLE LISTINGS

The grid contains the names of several cable TV networks and channels, past and present. The technology for cable TV started in 1948 when John Walson, an appliance store owner in a mountainous area of Pennsylvania, was having trouble selling TV sets to his neighbors because TV reception was poor due to nearby mountains blocking broadcast signals sent from big cities. But Mr. Walson was soon selling lots of TVs when reception improved dramatically. The hidden message tells what Mr. Walson did to solve the problem.

```
G  A  L  A  V  I  S  I  O  N  H
E  N  O  O  T  R  A  C  P  C  U
N  I  C  K  E  L  O  D  E  O  N
T  M  A  O  E  N  A  I  N  M  T
E  A  N  K  U  D  I  S  N  E  Y
N  L  I  N  A  R  U  C  P  D  O
N  P  A  H  I  S  T  O  R  Y  O
S  L  S  U  S  R  E  V  B  C  X
W  A  W  E  A  T  H  E  R  E  Y
E  N  B  O  O  M  E  R  A  N  G
N  E  N  A  P  S  C  Y  V  T  E
X  T  M  S  N  B  C  K  O  R  N
O  M  X  A  M  E  N  I  C  A  O
F  O  O  D  U  N  T  D  F  L  A
E  M  I  T  W  O  H  S  I  I  N
```

ANIMAL PLANET	FOX NEWS
BOOMERANG	GALAVISION
BRAVO	HISTORY
CARTOON	MSNBC
CINEMAX	NICKELODEON
COMEDY CENTRAL	OXYGEN
COURT [TV]	SCI FI
C-SPAN	SHOWTIME
DISCOVERY KIDS	SPIKE [TV]
DISNEY	VERSUS
ESPN	WEATHER
FOOD	

45. A MAN WITH GREAT PRESENTS

Shaped like a present with a bow on top, the grid contains words and phrases about Santa Claus. The hidden message is what Santa said to his wife about the weather on Christmas Eve—but which hurt the feelings of his sleigh-pulling team who heard it a different way.

```
      T O Y S           S U I T
    T           K   R           O
    E               E               M
  N L           T       E           R I
      V R T               H G S
  H R T I E O D S S K C I N T S
  W E U L S S O J O L L Y R E K
  O E E L A I K F A E E T S L O
  R D A M C V Y U T O P I I O I
  K N X D K E S A N O I M G P R
  S I T O N H I S L A P Y R H A
  H E I M A K I N G A L I S T N
  O R I D E W H I T E B E A R D
  P H P L O D U R S E I K O O C
  C A C O M I N G T O T O W N R
```

CHIMNEY	ROOFTOP
COMING TO TOWN	ROSY CHEEKS
COOKIES	RUDOLPH
ELVES	SACK
JOLLY	SIT ON HIS LAP
LETTERS	SLEIGH
MAKING A LIST	ST. NICK
MILK	SUIT
MRS. CLAUS	TOYS
NORTH POLE	WHITE BEARD
PIPE	WORKSHOP
REINDEER	XMAS

46. DOUBLE U'S

Each word below contains at least 2 U's. The same is true for the 3 U.S. cities located in the hidden message.

```
Y  N  A  N  L  U  Z  U  S  I  S
L  M  H  O  N  O  L  U  L  U  U
L  U  B  I  U  Q  O  U  R  E  B
A  T  R  T  E  U  Q  U  O  B  U
U  U  Q  A  T  U  A  U  E  D  R
T  A  U  R  U  S  R  U  L  U  B
U  T  I  U  O  U  K  O  D  U  S
M  V  C  G  G  L  U  X  U  R  Y
E  S  E  U  G  U  T  R  O  P  E
T  T  A  A  C  M  S  H  A  L  F
S  Y  T  N  N  U  D  U  E  D  U
U  U  U  I  B  C  M  L  A  U  T
G  Q  T  J  U  J  U  B  E  L  U
U  S  U  Z  U  K  I  U  E  E  R
A  C  U  P  U  N  C  T  U  R  E
```

ACUPUNCTURE	MUTUALLY
AUGUST	PORTUGUESE
AUTUMN	STEGOSAURUS
BOUQUET	SUBURBS
CUCUMBER	SUDOKU
CUMULUS	SUZUKI
FUTURE	TAURUS
HONOLULU	TUTU
INAUGURATION	UKULELE
ISUZU	URUGUAY
JUJUBE	USUAL
LUXURY	VIRTUOUS

47. IN THE BATHROOM

The grid contains things found in a bathroom. The hidden message answers this riddle: Why did the boy's mother tell him to go wash his face?

```
L  M  O  U  T  H  W  A  S  H  H
D  E  N  T  A  L  F  L  O  S  S
E  D  W  O  M  Y  G  A  S  I  H
V  I  E  O  H  S  H  E  H  N  A
H  C  D  P  T  O  T  C  O  K  V
H  I  L  M  A  L  O  E  W  E  I
A  N  I  A  B  M  L  H  E  T  N
I  E  M  H  B  R  C  S  R  S  G
R  C  A  S  D  I  H  U  C  A  C
D  A  Q  T  I  P  S  R  U  P  R
R  B  U  T  H  T  A  B  R  H  E
Y  I  R  T  Y  L  W  P  T  T  A
E  N  O  I  T  O  L  O  A  O  M
R  E  P  A  P  T  E  L  I  O  T
O  T  E  C  U  A  F  K  N  T  S
```

BATHMAT	MOUTHWASH
BATHTUB	Q-TIPS
BRUSH	SHAMPOO
COMB	SHAVING CREAM
DENTAL FLOSS	SHOWER CURTAIN
FAUCET	SINK
HAIR DRYER	SOAP
LOTION	TOILET PAPER
LYSOL	TOOTHPASTE
MEDICINE CABINET	TOWEL
MILDEW	WASHCLOTH

48. USE A PAINTBRUSH

Shaped like a paintbrush, the grid on the facing page contains words that can be created by rearranging the letters in PAINTBRUSH. Every word or phrase contains from 4 to 8 letters (from the 10 different letters in PAINTBRUSH) and no letter is ever repeated within a word. All the words in the hidden message also come from PAINTBRUSH and make up an unusual but not nonsensical sentence.

This puzzle is especially challenging because you'll be hunting for 60 items rather than the usual 20 to 25. When you're done, take an extra challenge and see how many more words you can form from the letters of PAINTBRUSH.

AIRBUS	INPUT	SHUT
AUSTIN	IRAN	SIT-UP
BANISH	NABS	SNUB
BARNS	NUTS	SPAIN
BASIN	PAIRS	SPRAIN
BATHS	PANTS	SPRINT
BIRTH	PARIS	SPURT
BRAINS	PATH	STIR UP
BRATS	PINT	SUBPAR
BURNT	PUNISH	SUIT
BURPS	PURITANS	TAPIR
BURST	RUIN	TARNISH
BUSH	RUST	THAN
HABITS	SAINT	TRASH
HAIR	SATIN	TUBAS
HARPIST	SATURN	TURBANS
HATPINS	SHARP	TURNIPS
HAUNT	SHIRT	UNIT
HINTS	SHRUB	UNSTRAP
HURT	SHUN	UTAH

```
            N H T
          S A I N T
          R B   U U
          U S   A R
          S I   H B
          T T T A A
          S A N B N
          P A R I S
          B I R T H
          A A R S S
          N A I U A
          I N P U T
          S N A A U
          H A T U R
        S T P N T N T
      A P U R I T A N S
    R H R R P R A H T T N
  T B I S N I P T A H U P U
  U T U H I T S R R S S H T
  S H A R P N B H P N U H S
  P I N U S P R A I N I A S
  A S A B U T T A S I T U P
  N U N N B A R I T I B T A
  T S I H P B A R N S N H I
  S S H A A I T B P H S A N
  H P A I R S A U S T I N U
  S I R R R N R S N A N P T
  U T R U H T N R U B I I S
  B   T   B   A   B   S   P
```

49. HANDY DANDY

The grid contains things you put on your hands, arms, fingers, or wrists. The hidden message names five very different kinds of gloves.

```
S  O  C  K  P  U  P  P  E  T  B
O  X  G  I  M  I  T  T  E  N  S
N  S  U  N  B  L  O  C  K  E  G
R  U  I  B  B  E  V  E  E  L  S
H  N  T  A  T  T  O  O  E  L  R
A  H  A  N  D  W  A  R  M  E  R
N  W  R  I  S  T  W  R  A  P  E
D  F  P  T  L  I  W  N  G  E  L
C  E  I  E  R  P  L  A  G  R  B
U  E  C  L  S  S  O  N  T  T  M
F  A  K  E  N  A  I  L  S  C  I
F  H  O  C  C  R  K  O  I  E  H
S  D  N  A  B  T  A  E  W  S  T
M  A  E  R  C  P  E  Y  O  N  H
V  E  N  B  B  A  N  D  A  I  D
```

BAND-AID	RING
BRACELET	SLEEVE
CREAM	SOAP
FAKE NAILS	SOCK PUPPET
GUITAR PICK	SUNBLOCK
HANDCUFFS	SWEATBAND
HANDWARMER	TATTOO
INSECT REPELLENT	THIMBLE
MITTENS	WATCH
NAIL POLISH	WRIST WRAP

50. CAN YOU CUT IT?

Shaped like a birthday cake with candles, the grid contains things that you cut. The hidden message is a definition of the phrase "cut the mustard."

```
        B     S     I     B     E
        G     T     T     I     C
        N     N     O     R     O
        I     A     U     T     R
  S  R  C  L  O  T  H  H  G  N  T
  E  T  E  P  R  A  C  D  W  E  H
  I  S  O  H  O  I  H  A  I  R  E
  T  A  P  E  W  D  L  Y  E  S  M
  L  A  E  D  A  N  O  C  W  U  U
  F  I  N  G  E  R  N  A  I  L  S
  P  A  P  E  R  G  L  K  R  U  T
  S  H  T  O  S  C  S  E  E  M  A
  U  M  E  A  T  O  C  C  E  B  R
  S  D  R  A  C  F  O  K  C  E  D
     E  C  D  S  S  A  L  C  R
```

A DEAL	LAWN
BIRTHDAY CAKE	LOOSE
CARPET	LUMBER
CAT CLAWS	MEAT
CLASS	PAPER
CLOTH	PLANTS
CORNERS	SANDWICH
DECK OF CARDS	STRING
FINGERNAILS	TAPE
HAIR	THE MUSTARD
HEDGE	TIES
IT OUT	WIRE

51. YOU'RE ALL WET

Shaped like a water balloon, the grid contains things you'll find water in. The hidden message tells with a rhyme what'll happen if a water balloon splats on some warm-up clothes.

```
              A     I
              Q
        T  B  L  U  W
     B  U  T  H  T  A  B
     V  C  L  G  T  U  T  R  R
  G  K  A  L  A  K  E  E  R  I  E
N  E  N  A  S  Q  U  I  R  T  G  U  N
T  Y  S  I  A  E  S  W  B  R  M  P  M
P  S  L  L  A  F  A  R  A  G  A  I  N
U  E  S  O  H  T  E  I  L  A  E  T  T
D  R  S  P  R  I  N  K  L  E  R  C  L
D  S  H  P  I  S  S  U  O  N  T  H  A
L  W  O  B  T  E  L  I  O  T  S  E  N
E  N  U  O  Y  A  B  O  N  F  H  R  A
D  R  R  T  O  P  G  N  I  K  O  O  C
T  M  I  T  N  A  T  L  O  O  W  A  W
   E  T  L  L  S  L  O  O  P  E  H
      R  E  S  E  R  V  O  I  R
         W  B  I  R  T
```

AQUARIUM	GLASS	RESERVOIR
BATHTUB	HOSE	SHOWER
BAYOU	LAGOON	SINK
BOTTLE	LAKE ERIE	SPRINKLER
BROOK	NIAGARA FALLS	SQUIRT GUN
BUCKET	PITCHER	STREAM
CANAL	POND	TOILET BOWL
COOKING POT	POOL	VASE
FOUNTAIN	PUDDLE	WATER BALLOON
GEYSER	RAINSTORM	WELL

52. YOU BIG APE!

Shaped like one movie version of the top of the Empire State Building, the grid contains things from the *King Kong* movies. The hidden message tells the surprising size of the models that were used to create the giant ape in the original version of the movie back in 1933.

```
                    G
                    N
                    I
                    D
                    L
              E  I  J
              T  U  H
              N  B  C
        C  G  E  E  E  S  Y
     W  L  A  E  T  R  R  E  E
  Y  E  S  E  P  A  C  S  E  R  R
  T  T  R  M  C  T  M  E  V  A  G
  U  R  U  Y  A  S  U  E  O  L  N
  A  Y  A  E  I  E  P  R  L  G  O
  E  W  S  H  T  R  R  A  E  E  K
E  N  B  I  O  F  F  I  L  C  N  D  G  N  C
H  U  S  E  N  A  L  P  I  B  S  D  N  E  S
S  S  B  M  I  L  C  M  H  I  G  P  I  H  S
B  L  O  N  D  E  N  E  W  Y  O  R  K  K  H
```

BEAST	JUNGLE
BEAUTY	KIDNAP
BIPLANES	KING KONG
BLONDE	LOVE
CAPTURED	NEW YORK
CLIFF	RESCUE
CLIMBS	ROAR
DINOSAURS	SCREAMS
EMPIRE STATE BUILDING	SHIP
ESCAPE	SUBWAY CAR

53. GETTING IN THE LAST WORDS

The word LAST can come before every item in the word list to form a common word or phrase, like LAST BUT NOT LEAST or LAST CHANCE. All these items are hidden in this last grid, which is shaped from the block letters L-A-S-T. The hidden message is a little poem that expresses how we hope you feel about this book.

```
  I  T  E                 W  G  E
  W  N  T              R  A  E  Y  O
  O  B  U           T  S  E  M  A  N  J
  N  U  N           P  T        E  U
  K  T  I           B  R  H  C  T  I  D
  O  N  M  A  N  S  T  A  N  D  I  N  G
  T  O  Y  I  U  C  R  W        T  M
  N  T  F  P  L  R  H  A        O  E
S  O  L  P  T  U  E     A  N  L  O  T  N  W
W  S  E  Y  H  O  U     R  N  I  G  H  T  E
O  R  A                 C  D  E
R  E  S  O  R  T  O      K  E  P
D  P  T  E  N  E  T      S  C  O
         T  I  A         T  N  O
H  T  N  O  M  I  L      A  A  L
F  O  R  E  V  E  R      S  D  T
```

BUT NOT LEAST	MONTH
CHANCE	NAME
DANCE	NIGHT
DITCH	ONE INTO THE POOL...
FOREVER	PERSON TO KNOW
GASP	RESORT
HURRAH	RITES
JUDGMENT	STRAW
LICKS	SUPPER
MAN STANDING	TIME
MILE	WORD
MINUTE	YEAR

Answers

WORD LISTS

24. ALL TOGETHER NOW

1. BURGER and FRIES
2. CATS and DOGS
3. DOLLARS and CENTS
4. LADIES and GENTLEMEN
5. READ and WRITE
6. RISE and SHINE
7. SOCKS and SHOES
8. STARS and STRIPES
9. TABLE and CHAIR
10. WISHING and HOPING

39. WORD CHAIN

1. PHOTOGRAPH
2. HOSPITAL
3. LIGHTNING
4. GALAXY
5. YELLOW
6. WONDERFUL
7. LAPTOP
8. PUBLIC
9. CONFETTI
10. INVESTIGATION
11. NUTRITIOUS
12. SABBATH
13. HIPPO
14. OGRE
15. EXCELLENT
16. THUMB
17. BULLDOZER
18. REIGNED
19. DRUM
20. MYSTERY
21. YANKEE
22. EGGS
23. SOLVING
24. GOLF
25. FUMBLE

1. IN FIRST PLACE

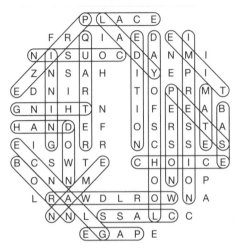

Finished "In First Place"

2. WORD SEARCH WORD SEARCH

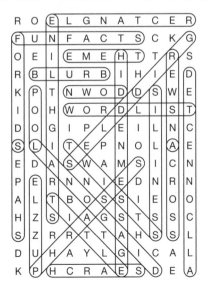

Rocket ship, iPod, and birthday cake

3. TREE-MENDOUS

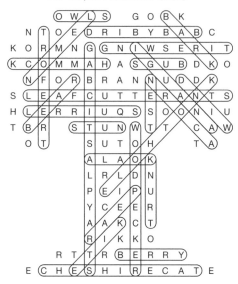

Go knock on a door and shout out, "Trick or tree!"

4. LISTEN UP!

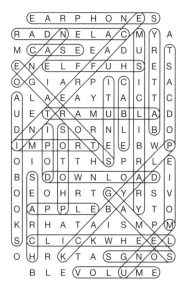

A media player with ports that is portable

5. OUT TO LAUNCH

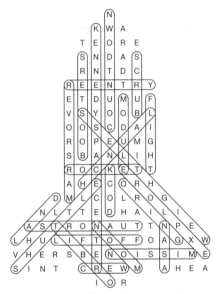

A treadmill that hovers in the air

6. COLOR-FULL

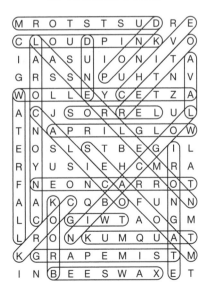

Rising sun, just blush, aqua mint

7. YIKES!

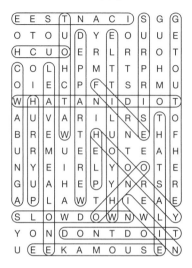

"Go to your room this minute!"
"I hate you!"

8. FINGER FOOD

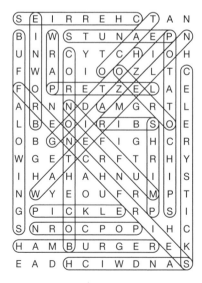

Anything bigger than your head

9. HEADRESTS

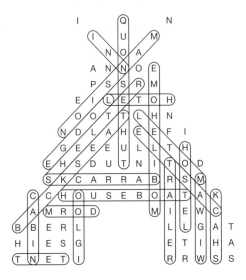

In an open field under the stars

10. TALKING ANIMALS

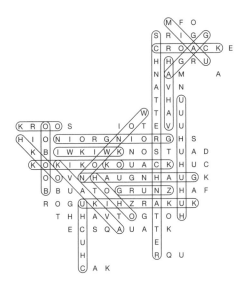

For Germans, it is not a duck but a frog that goes "Quak-Quak!"

11. FALL IN LINE

Old Wives' Summer or All-Hallown Summer
[which is related to Halloween]

12. BE A GOOD SPORT

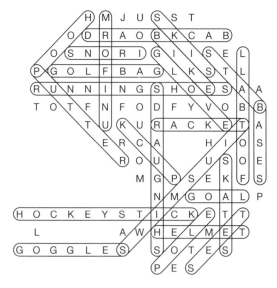

Just eat off of your home plate.

13. ANIMATED MOVIES

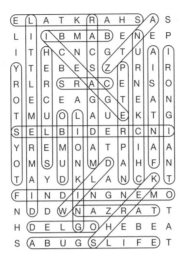

Sleeping Beauty and the Beast

14. DO YOU FOLLOW ME?

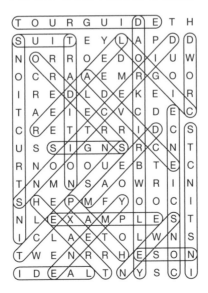

They produce more leaders, not more followers.

15. IN A PET STORE

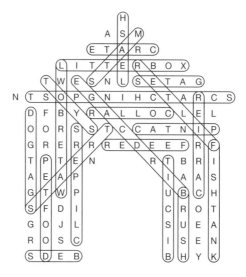

An NFL or NBA dog jersey

16. STAR SEARCH

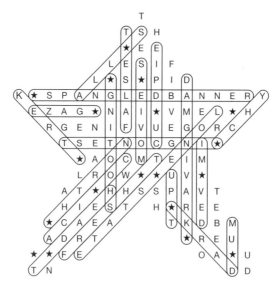

The five-<u>star</u> general was the be<u>st ar</u>ound.

17. FROM A TO Z

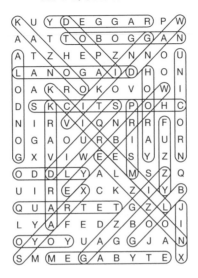

Up at the zoo, a roving ox was quickly fed bug jam.

18. ACHOO!

Almost everybody closes their eyes.

19. WHAT I GO THROUGH

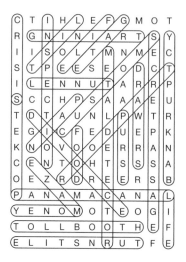

The motions, a change, the roof

20. JUST BEAT IT

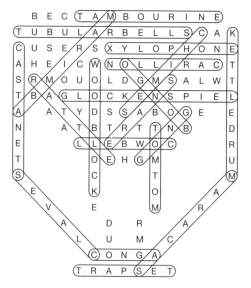

Because she could always beat the drum

21. OPEN UP!

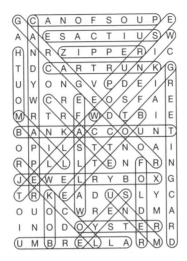

A conversation and your mind

22. WORKING LATE

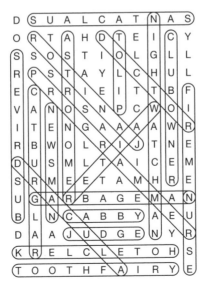

Do they still say, "Let's call it a day"?

23. RING-A-DING-DING

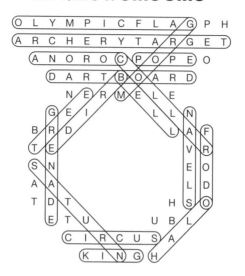

Phone, bathtub

24. ALL TOGETHER NOW

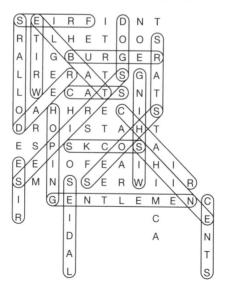

In the Together States of America

25. A WORK OF ART

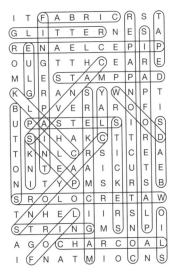

It's not the materials…it's the imagination.

26. GLASS

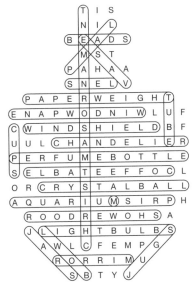

Is it half full or half empty?

27. SIGNS AHEAD

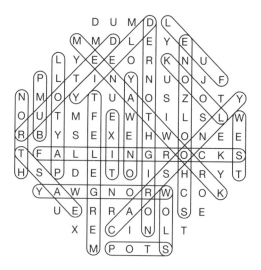

Dummy! You just missed your exit!

28. LOST IN CYBERSPACE

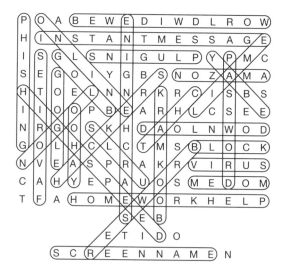

A cyberspace space station

29. PLAYING PINBALL

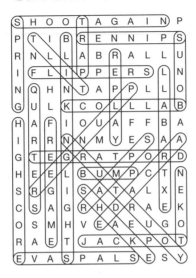

Pinball Hall of Fame, Las Vegas

30. TOP-OF-THE-LINE

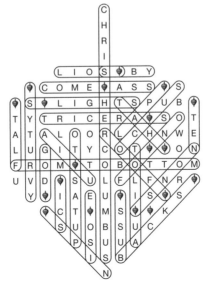

Blow your top.

31. IT'S ABOUT TIME

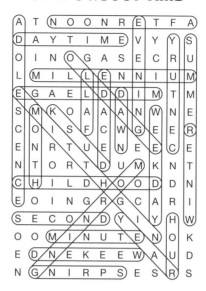

Tying a score or undoing crookedness
[These are two other definitions of EVENING.]

32. MAPS, DNA, AND SPAM

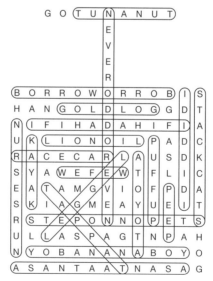

Go hang a salami. I'm a lasagna hog.

33. TAKE A WALK

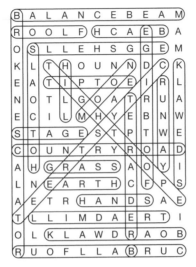

A mountain trail

34. SOUNDS FAMILIAR

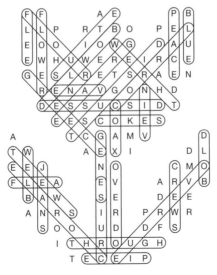

A prophet and a maid made a profit.

35. FOR GOOD MEASURE

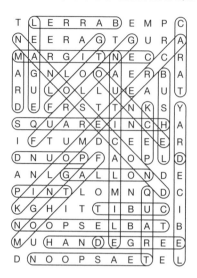

Temperature, latitude, and longitude

36. ALL AROUND AFRICA

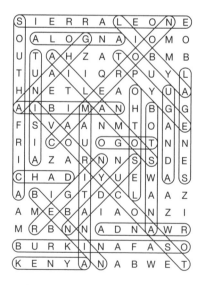

Mozambique, Tanzania, Zambia, Zimbabwe

37. WHAT'S THAT IN THE SKY?

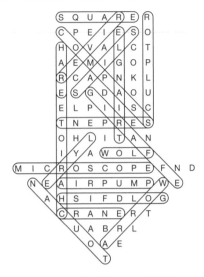

Peacock, Dolphin, and Table

38. SEUSS IN USE

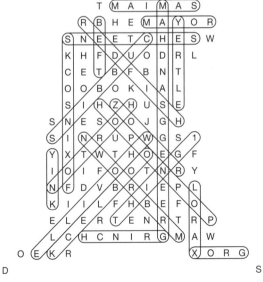

The whole book contains just fifty different words.

39. WORD CHAIN

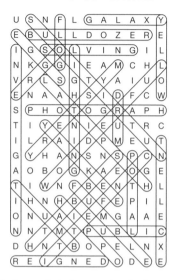

Unlike a chain, a circle has no beginning and no end.

40. THOSE WHO SERVE

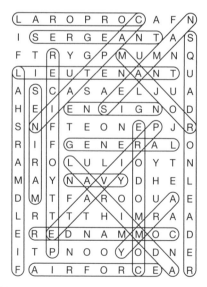

A fifty-gun salute on July the Fourth at noon

41. AT HOME PLATE

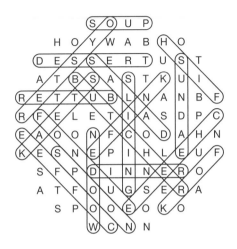

How about a tablespoon plus a teaspoon?

42. THE IN CROWD

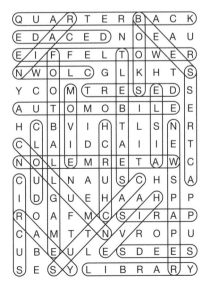

Naughty child in a heap of trouble

43. RHYME TIME

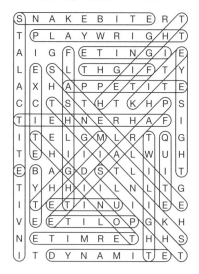

Right headlight

44. CABLE LISTINGS

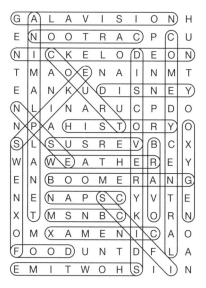

He put an antenna up on a mountain.

45. A MAN WITH GREAT PRESENTS

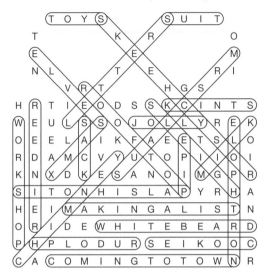

Tonight I'd sure like to avoid any rain, dear. [reindeer]

46. DOUBLE U'S

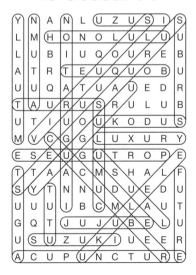

Albuquerque, Duluth, and Dubuque
[in New Mexico, Minnesota, and Iowa]

47. IN THE BATHROOM

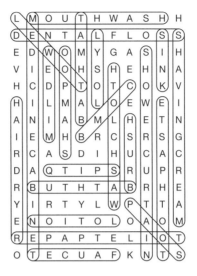

He gave her a dirty look.

48. USE A PAINTBRUSH

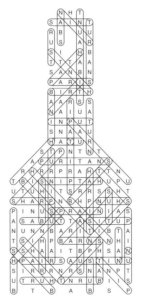

His Aunt Pat puts thin tuna bits in pitas.

49. HANDY DANDY

Boxing, rubber, fingerless, hockey, oven

50. CAN YOU CUT IT?

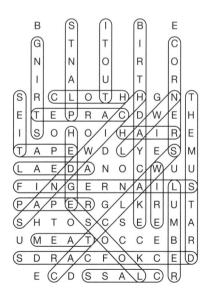

Be good enough to succeed.

51. YOU'RE ALL WET

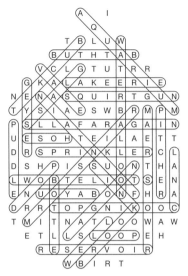

It'll turn a sweatshirt into a wet shirt.

52. YOU BIG APE!

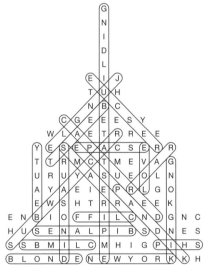

They were merely eighteen inches high.

53. GETTING IN THE LAST WORDS

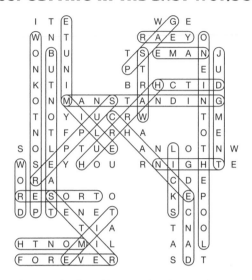

It went by fast. Now you're done at last.

Index

Italics indicate answer page number

About the Author

Mark Danna earns his living writing puzzles: more than 20 word search books; the newspaper-syndicated, rhymes-with-clues *Wordy Gurdy*; American Mensa's annual page-a-day calendar *365 Brain Puzzlers*; and some 200 crosswords, including Sundays in *The New York Times*. Danna has been an associate editor at *Games* magazine and a staff writer for *Who Wants to Be a Millionaire*. To order personalized word searches, crosswords, or other puzzles, contact Mark at puzzlestogo@gmail.com.

Also by Mark Danna